Published in 2020 by Enslow Publishing, LLC.
101 W. 23rd Street, Suite 240, New York, NY 10011

Copyright © 2020 by Enslow Publishing, LLC.

All rights reserved.

No part of this book may be reproduced by any means without the written permission of the publisher.

Library of Congress Cataloging-in-Publication Data

Names: Hagler, Gina, author.
Title: Earth science in your everyday life / Gina Hagler.
Description: New York : Enslow Publishing, 2020. | Series: Real world science | Includes bibliographical references and index. | Audience: Grade 5 to 8.
Identifiers: LCCN 2018049653 | ISBN 9781978507609 (library bound) | ISBN 9781978509474 (pbk.)
Subjects: LCSH: Earth sciences—Juvenile literature.
Classification: LCC QE29.H137 2020 | DDC 550—dc23
LC record available at https://lccn.loc.gov/2018049653

Printed in the United States of America

To Our Readers: We have done our best to make sure all website addresses in this book were active and appropriate when we went to press. However, the author and the publisher have no control over and assume no liability for the material available on those websites or on any websites they may link to. Any comments or suggestions can be sent by email to customerservice@enslow.com.

Photo Credits: Cover, p. 1 Tom Wang/Shutterstock.com; cover, p. 1 (science icons), back cover pattern kotoffei/Shutterstock.com; cover, p. 1 (globe graphic) Elkersh/Shutterstock.com; cover, interior pages (circular pattern) John_Dakapu/Shutterstock.com; p. 5 EpicStockMedia/Shutterstock.com; p. 6 JVrublevskaya/Shutterstock.com; p. 8 Sakurra/Shutterstock.com; p. 10 U.S. Geological Survey/Getty Images; p. 12 Peter Hermes Furian/Shutterstock.com; p. 14 Santhosh Varghese/Shutterstock.com; p. 18 Rainer Lesniewski/Shutterstock.com; p. 20 (top) milosk50/Shutterstock.com; p. 20 (bottom) Josef Hanus/Shutterstock.com; p. 23 Harvepino/Shutterstock.com; p. 24 Multiverse/Shutterstock.com; pp. 29, 52 Designua/Shutterstock.com; p. 31 Minerva Studio/Shutterstock.com; p. 33 Chz_mhOng/Shutterstock.com; p. 35 Gina Hagler Shutterstock.com; p. 40 BlueRingMedia/Shutterstock.com; p. 41 mapichai/Shutterstock.com; p. 44 Frances Roberts/Alamy Stock Photo; p. 48 Nerdist72/Shutterstock.com; p. 50 VectorMine/Shutterstock.com.

Contents

Introduction 4

■ **Chapter 1**
The Earth Beneath Your Feet 7

■ **Chapter 2**
The Oceans Around You 17

■ **Chapter 3**
Let's Talk About the Weather 28

■ **Chapter 4**
The Earth-Sun-Moon System 38

■ **Chapter 5**
Cycles in Action 47

Chapter Notes 58
Glossary 61
Further Reading 62
Index 63

Introduction

Earth science is all around us. We see it in action during earthquakes and volcanoes. It is the science that helps us understand the "why" behind these scientific events. It is also the science behind processes such as erosion that are less obvious at first glance. Earth science is comprised of several different fields that focus on an aspect of the way Earth and its systems behave. Geology is the study of the composition of Earth. Oceanography is the study of the oceans. Meteorology is the study of Earth's atmosphere, including the weather. Astronomy focuses on the universe and the effects of bodies in the universe upon our planet.

But none of these areas of study work independently of the others. Each is involved in one or more cycles, such as the water cycle, that must remain in balance if life on Earth is to thrive.

You don't have to be a scientist to see evidence of the processes in the fields of earth science. The rocks we build with and the minerals we consume are part of geology. Fossil fuels that fuel our cars and heat our homes are also part of this field of science. When we're at the shore, we see oceanography in action. We see the effect that the waves have on the sand on the beach. We feel the undertow and notice the way the sand around our feet is moved by the water. High-pressure and low-pressure fronts influence the weather. The heat on the pavement causes convection currents that rise in the air and provide hawks and other birds with an easier ride. The phases of the moon help us understand the motion of Earth. The behavior of the tides gives us a look at the influence of the moon on our planet. Each of these events leads us to a deeper understanding of earth science.

Introduction

Oceanography includes examining the forces that cause motion, such as how the wind blowing across the ocean creates waves. The stronger the winds, the bigger the waves.

Earth Science in Your Everyday Life

Coal can be mined from a quarry. This coal is being loaded for transport. In the United States, coal is mainly used as fuel to generate electricity.

By learning about the fields of earth science, examining issues of current interest, and experimenting with the theories we've learned, we can make choices about things such as what type of fuel to use and what type of packaging is most ecologically sound—decisions that are important to the health of Earth itself.

The Earth Beneath Your Feet

Chapter 1

At the most basic level, geology is the science of cooling, settling, and eroding. Earth has four layers of material. It includes the crust and mantle, as well as the outer and inner cores. You may not realize it at first, but in the same way that Earth's crust rests on the layers below, the waters of Earth's oceans do as well. Volcanoes, the way the continents form a sort of jigsaw puzzle, and earthquakes are evidence of geological processes happening all around us.

Crust, Mantle, Core

A solid core about 759 miles (1,221.5 kilometers) thick sits at the very center of Earth. Temperatures there can reach 9,300°F (5,149°C). This solid core is surrounded by a liquid outer core that has a radius of about 1,400 miles (2,253 km). Temperatures there are about 10,800°F (5,982°C). This makes it about as hot as the surface of the sun. Both these cores are made of iron and nickel, which are in solid form in the inner core and liquid form in the outer core.

The mantle is next, with temperatures that range from about 7,230°F (4,000°C) near the outer core to roughly 700°F (371°C) on average just beneath the crust. This is the thickest layer at about 1,774 miles (2,855 km) thick. This thick liquid layer is so hot that rock exists in molten form. The crust is the layer we are most familiar with. It is about 21 miles (34 km) thick on land. There is a

Earth Science in Your Everyday Life

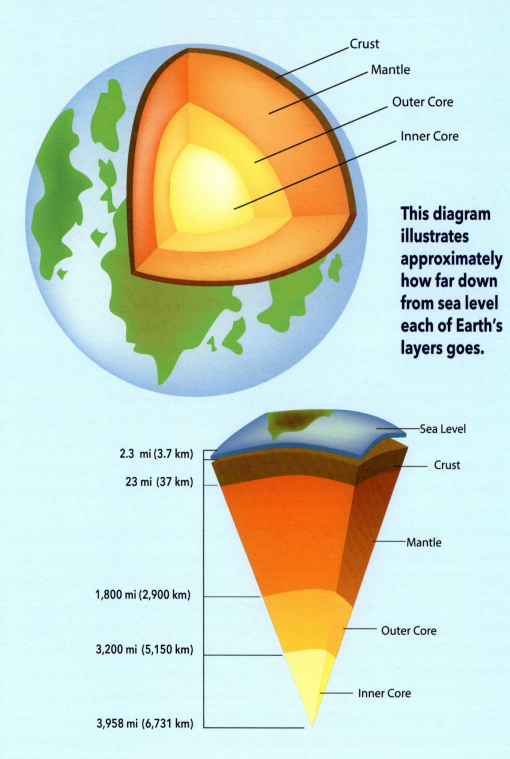

This diagram illustrates approximately how far down from sea level each of Earth's layers goes.

8

crust beneath the ocean, too. It is only about 3 miles (5 km) thick. The temperature at the crust ranges from about 752°F (400°C) where it meets the mantle to 200°F (93°C) at the surface. Soil and other geological features such as mountains sit atop this. All of the geological activity we observe occurs as a result of activity at one of these levels.[1]

Fossil Fuels

Most cars, trucks, and buses on the road today use fossil fuels. These fuels use the energy in oil, coal, and natural gas that formed from the decomposition of dead plants and organisms beneath the ground. For instance, an animal may have died in a lake or sea millions of years ago. The body decomposed, and the organic matter that resulted mixed with mud and sank deeper. Additional layers of sediment settled upon that layer. Over time, pressure and heat caused a chemical transformation. The result was liquid and gaseous hydrocarbon molecules. On land, decomposing plants formed coal and methane. We make the gas we need to run our vehicles and the fuel we need to heat our homes from these fossil fuels. They are nonrenewable, so there is a move toward solar power and wind power—renewable sources—to generate the electricity we need to run our homes and businesses.[2]

Volcanic Activity

A volcano is the result of lava from the mantle rising through an opening in Earth's crust. There are two main types of volcanoes. Shield volcanoes are generally found in the middle of tectonic plates. There is a "bowl" in the middle. The Kilauea volcano on the Big Island of Hawaii is of this type. Composite volcanoes are the type you are probably more used to seeing. These have a cone shape and spew out rocks and other material along with

Earth Science in Your Everyday Life

The Pu'u 'Ō'ō crater on the Kilauea volcano collapsed on April 30, 2018, igniting an eruption that lasted for months. About 1,700 residents had to evacuate, and about 700 homes were destroyed.

ash. The volcano at Mount St. Helens in the state of Washington is a great example of this type.

The lava from a volcano begins as magma when it is beneath the surface of Earth. When the magma and gases build up pressure, the magma must go somewhere. As this magma flows out on the surface, we call it lava. The lava is able to escape the volcano in several ways. When the lava is thin, as is the case with a shield volcano, the gases escape and the lava flows. When the lava is thick, as in a composite volcano, the gas is not able to escape. It builds pressure until there is enough to fracture the rock surrounding the flow. When this happens, and pressure builds enough, the lava and gas erupt in the same way a bottle of fizzy liquid does when it is shaken.

The Ring of Fire

The Ring of Fire is a series of volcanoes around the Pacific Ocean that form a horseshoe shape from New Zealand to Indonesia, Japan, and Russia on the west to Alaska and the west coasts of North, Central, and South America. Most of Earth's volcanoes are located here because of the ability of magma to escape the mantle through the motion of Earth's plates.

Twelve of the volcanoes in this ring are considered dangerous because they have the potential for massive destruction. The countries in greatest potential danger from these volcanoes are Japan, the Philippines, and Indonesia. Of those, Japan is considered to be a top spot in the world for seismic activity such as volcanoes and earthquakes.[3]

Earth Science in Your Everyday Life

Plate Tectonics

If you look at a map of Earth, you'll notice that several of the continents look as if they could fit together in a jigsaw puzzle. Geologists also noticed this. Their research indicates that there was once one large continent they call the Pangea supercontinent. Their research also indicates that Pangea broke into parts due to the action of plate tectonics.

Tectonic plates are part of the lithosphere—the crust and part of the upper mantle. They are resting on the mantle and the material beneath the mantle. As the plates were formed, the land

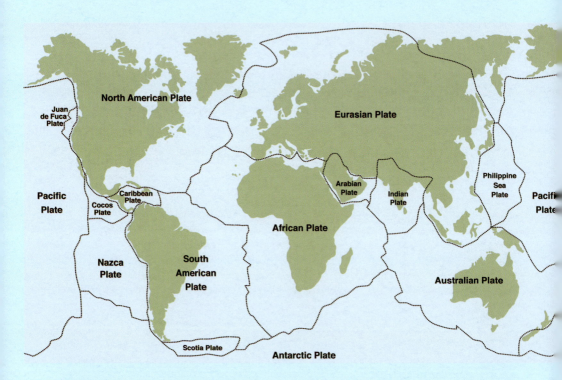

This plate tectonic map shows the major and minor plates located beneath the continents and oceans. The Pacific plate is the largest at 39,768,522 square miles (103,000,000 km^2).

above them moved with the plate beneath it. Over time, the result is the arrangement of continents you see today.[4]

Earthquakes

Earthquakes are one way we know that there are plates in movement beneath the surface we stand on. When plates bump into one another, they cause seismic activity. We don't feel every slight movement, but we do feel the results when two blocks of earth slipping past one another produce enough energy for that energy to be radiated to the surface. The place where this activity occurs is called a fault.

The greatest force from an earthquake is felt at its epicenter, the place where the plates moved. The "shock" from the earthquake spreads out in a ring like the one around a rock you throw into the water. Just as with the rock and water, the larger the shock, the greater the disruption. Scientists can measure the magnitude of an earthquake with a seismometer, but they cannot predict when one will occur. They do know that earthquakes are most likely to occur above a fault.[5]

Activity: Building an Erupting Volcano

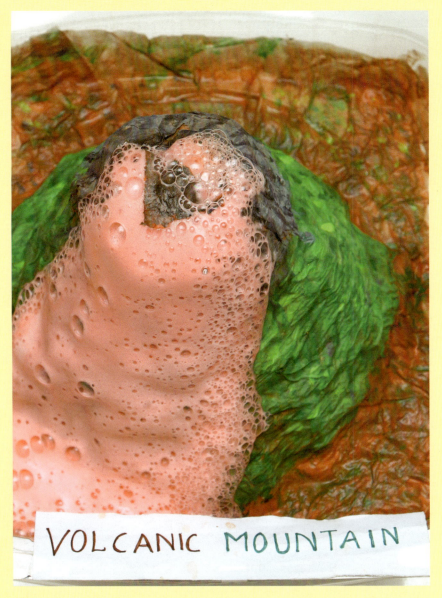

The foam created by mixing baking soda and vinegar in this model volcano simulates the lava flowing from a real volcano during an eruption.

The Earth Beneath Your Feet

This activity has two steps.

Step 1. Fill a balloon with gas.
You could just get a helium tank, but let's use what you know about volcanoes to fill the balloon.

Things You Will Need:

- goggles
- a balloon
- 2 oz (59 mL) of water
- a 12-oz (355-mL) bottle with a narrow top, clean and empty
- 1 teaspoon (5 grams) of baking soda
- something long enough to stir the liquid
- a few tablespoons of lemon juice

■ **1.** Put your goggles on.
■ **2.** Stretch the balloon a bit so it is easier to fill.
■ **3.** Pour the water into the empty bottle.
■ **4.** Add the baking soda and stir to dissolve in the water.
■ **5.** Pour the lemon juice in.
■ **6.** QUICKLY stretch the mouth of the balloon over the top of the bottle.

Is your balloon inflating? What created the gas? Why is the gas filling the balloon? How does this apply to what you know about gases in the magma beneath Earth's crust?

The baking soda mixing with the lemon juice created the gas. The gas built up in the bottle and escaped into the balloon, filling it up. The gases beneath the crust also build up and need to escape.

Earth Science in Your Everyday Life

Step 2. Make a volcano.
Now apply what you know about creating a gas with what you know about erupting volcanoes.

Things You Will Need:

- goggles
- a 25-oz (739-mL) bottle with a narrow top, clean and empty
- paper towels
- a big bowl for the liquids that will erupt from your volcano
- a plastic tablecloth (or go outside)
- 1½ cups (355 mL) of warm water
- food coloring
- 2 tablespoons (28 g) of baking soda
- 1 cup (237 mL) of vinegar

■ 1. Put your goggles on.
■ 2. Wrap the sides of the bottle with paper towels so that it looks like a volcano. Stand it in the large bowl. Place the bowl on the tablecloth or take it outside.
■ 3. Pour the warm water into the bottle.
■ 4. Add several drops of food coloring.
■ 5. Put the baking soda into the water.
■ 6. Pour vinegar into the solution.
■ 7. Step back!

   Has the liquid come out of the bottle? Is it bubbling? What does the gas in the mixture have to do with a volcano?
   The vinegar mixing with the baking soda created gas. The gas built up until the pressure was so great, it erupted out of the bottle like a volcano.

The Oceans Around You

Chapter 2

Oceanography is the study of marine environments. It is not only about the oceans; it is about large bodies of fresh water, too. The water in the oceans sits atop the crust, just as the soil and features on solid ground do. The big difference is that the crust under the oceans is only about 3 miles (5 km) deep. Much of what occurs in the field of oceanography occurs beneath the surface of the ocean, but there are still many processes that have results you can see every day.

Currents

An ocean current is the continuous movement of water in a particular direction. You'll find currents flowing globally and locally. You'll find them near the surface and deep beneath the waves.

Currents are impacted by several things. The Coriolis effect of Earth's movement is one. It makes it impossible for a current to travel in a straight line; all currents have some sort of curve to them. It's also the reason that currents in the Southern Hemisphere move to the left while those in the Northern Hemisphere move to the right. Features on the ocean bottom also play a part since the current has to move around any tall areas and sinks into low areas.

The temperatures of surface currents and deep ocean currents help control the temperature of the land nearby. The water in the ocean also cycles because some water is saltier than other water. When this salty water is cold, it sinks to the bottom. As it heats up, it rises. This is what keeps the ocean from stagnating. You can see this for yourself when you observe the ocean. The water is salty and clear.

Earth Science in Your Everyday Life

The Gulf Stream influences the weather on the east coast of North America, as well as the west coast of Europe.

The Oceans Around You

The Gulf Stream is a major current in the Atlantic Ocean. Warm water moves along the coast of Florida, up to North Carolina, and northeast along the Atlantic Ocean, where it combines with other smaller currents to reach the area near Newfoundland. This current moves more water than is carried by all the rivers of the world combined. We feel its effect as far away as the climates of Ireland and Great Britain, where the temperatures on the west sides of those countries are warmer than the east sides. It also warms the air that reaches the Scandinavian mountains.[1]

Rip Currents

Rip currents are the most noticeable currents to us because they are on the surface and close to the shore. Sometimes there will be warnings when you go to the beach because these currents are not obvious to swimmers. The currents are made by water moving quickly away from the shore. It is usually in a "channel" that is 10 or 20 feet (3 to 6 meters) wide. You'll find rip currents along the coast at beaches with waves that break at the shore. The current begins close in and moves the swimmer out past the surf zone into deeper water. Because of the water moving out from the beach, the swimmer cannot swim back the way they came. Swimmers need to move parallel to the beach until they are clear of the rip current, then swim back to the beach.[2]

Tides

Tides are another noticeable process that is part of the study of the oceans. You'll notice the tide when you spend the day at the ocean. During a twenty-four-hour period, there are two high tides, spaced about twelve hours apart, and two low tides, also about twelve hours apart. When the tide is high, the water will be the farthest up the shore. Where waves were breaking, you will

Earth Science in Your Everyday Life

These images are of the same view of the Bay of Fundy. You can see the tremendous difference between low (*top*) and high tide.

The Oceans Around You

The Bay of Fundy

The highest high tide in the world is found in Nova Scotia, Canada, at the Bay of Fundy. The difference between high and low tide there is about 38 feet (12 m). That's a significant difference when you consider that a boat floating in water at high tide can be left high and dry at low tide. When the tide changes and the water rushes into the bay through the Minas Channel, the force of the water is equal to the power of eight thousand train engines or twenty-five million horses. The movement of so much water at such a force stirs everything around. The result is plenty of food for ocean life.[3]

see much calmer water. When tides are low, you will notice more beach is visible. The beach usually slopes down until the level of the water. You'll see rocks and shells down close to the water. This sloping portion of the beach is where you were standing when the tide was full. The tides are also an example of the effect of other celestial bodies upon Earth. In this particular instance, it is the moon that is exerting its gravitational pull upon the waters of our oceans. The difference in high and low tides is usually not extreme.[4]

Tropical Storms and Hurricanes

The temperature of the ocean does more than influence our climate. It also acts as a breeding ground for tropical storms and hurricanes. In the Atlantic Ocean, warm ocean waters combine

Earth Science in Your Everyday Life

with tropical disturbances to form the swirling storms we know as hurricanes. The warm ocean water provides energy for the storm. The winds of the storm need to be constant as they move upward into the sky.

Once a storm becomes a hurricane, it will move up the coast of North America or into the Gulf of Mexico. Some hurricanes make landfall and come ashore in southern states such as Florida or Texas. Depending on the wind speed, these hurricanes can cause tremendous damage. There will be warnings up and down the coast as people prepare their homes and businesses for the potential arrival of the hurricane and the especially high tides that come with it. If the hurricane is especially powerful, people who live near the coast or on barrier islands will be evacuated to shelters inland or on higher ground. Some hurricanes never come ashore. They remain over the ocean, moving north until the cooler waters of the mid-Atlantic slow them down and then rob them completely of their energy.

Global climate change is also having an effect on hurricanes. As the water temperatures rise in the ocean, hurricanes become larger and stronger. They also have a tendency in recent years to come ashore and stall. Very large rainfalls result from these large storms that stay in place. In recent years, more damage has been done by the fresh water flooding after the storm than from the winds or storm surge.[5]

Beaches After the Storm

You can see the effect of a hurricane or large storm on the beach the day after the event. You'll see more driftwood and other debris up on the beach. This material has come from other parts of the coast or in from the ocean. The debris makes it clear that a great deal of water has moved with great force during the storm.

The Oceans Around You

Hurricane Matthew travels along the Florida coastline in 2016. A hurricane viewed from space has a swirl with an eye in the center. In the Northern Hemisphere, the swirl rotates counterclockwise. In the Southern Hemisphere, it spins clockwise.

Earth Science in Your Everyday Life

Hurricane Irma decimated a boardwalk in Philipsburg, the capital of Saint Maarten in the Caribbean in 2017. A hurricane's strong winds and high tides not only cause damage, they also scatter debris along the coast.

It's exciting to visit the beach after the storm and see what you can find. It also gives you a chance to see the results of the ocean in action.

Hurricanes, storms, and tides also have a lasting effect on Earth's coastlines. The movement of the water wears away at rocky shores over generations. It pulls sand from sandy beaches back into the water on a daily basis. After a hurricane, it's not unusual to see that a beach is "smaller": there is less dry area than before the storm. The sand that formed the beach before the storm is still there, but it is farther out from the shore. In areas that have frequent tropical storms and hurricanes, it is often difficult to maintain a buffer between the ocean and houses that sit nearby.[6]

Activity: Comparing Beach Reclamation Methods

The action of the tides and the movement of water through currents, rip currents, and storms have an impact on the shoreline. Over time, great amounts of sand are moved from the shore into the ocean. The loss of land from these processes can be a serious problem for towns that attract summer crowds to their beaches. Also, if a house is built on a bluff at the coast, the action of the water can eat away at the base of the bluff. Similarly, as beaches erode, towns and homes at the shore have less of a buffer between them and the storm surges that occur during hurricanes and tropical storms.

Beach reclamation is the process of adding sand to the area that lost it because of erosion. It restores the shoreline to how it was before the movement of water moved the sand into the ocean.

Things You Will Need:

- **internet access**
- **a spreadsheet program such as Excel or a word processor with table option**

■ **1.** Find at least two methods for beach reclamation. Find one beach for each method.

■ **2.** Are the methods equally effective? Why would a town choose one method over another?

■ **3.** Give the pros and cons of the two types of beach reclamation. You may create a spreadsheet or table on your computer to organize the information. For example:

The Oceans Around You

	Pros	Cons
Method 1		
Method 2		

Let's Talk About the Weather

Meteorology is the study of the atmosphere, the things that happen in the atmosphere, and the ways in which those things affect the weather on Earth. It is this branch of earth science that makes it possible to forecast the weather. You experience the effects of meteorological events every day whether it is rain while you're walking home from school or a strong wind blowing as you get ready for bed. You also use the output of meteorology when you check the weather for the weekend before making plans. On a more direct level, you make judgments about the weather by looking at the sky.

Causes of Weather

Two key factors play a vital role in the weather. One is the temperature of Earth's surface in different locations. The other is the heating of the atmosphere closest to Earth's surface. Sometimes you can see that the air is "shimmering" as it rises off the hot pavement. Other times, you can see dark clouds skimming across the sky. Both are ways you directly observe the effects of Earth's heating or changes in atmospheric conditions.

Much of our weather is based upon air masses. These large masses of air are named according to their temperature and water vapor content. Air masses react to the surface conditions beneath them. They also cause changes of their own. When a large area of cold air moves in from the north, the temperature drops. When a warm air mass moves up from the south, you feel it as warmer

Let's Talk About the Weather

Cold front

Warm front

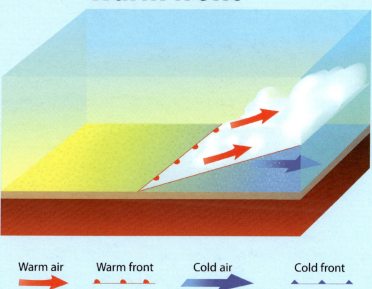

Cold air passing through warm air causes the air to become colder and drier. Warm air passing through cold air causes the air to become warmer and more humid.

Earth Science in Your Everyday Life

temperatures. We also feel it when a humid air mass moves in from the coast or a dry air mass comes in from the west.

When two air masses with different characteristics meet, the space between them is called a front. When you are in this transition zone, you can feel the change if you pay close attention. Sometimes the wind will change direction. Sometimes the temperature will be noticeably cooler in one place than in another. Sometimes you will be able to feel the humidity in the air rising or falling as you travel from one town to another.

It's even possible that you will drive a few miles and experience cloudy weather at the starting point, sun showers or drenching rains in the middle of the trip, and bright sunshine at the end point. This happens because you have traveled from one air mass, through the turbulent area between masses, and into a different air mass.[1]

Sometimes air masses move rapidly through an area. Other times the air mass stays in a region for a month or more. The masses get their start in an area where conditions on the surface are uniform, usually in a place that is flat. There are often light winds at the surface. The air masses can cover thousands of square miles. When an air mass is in place, the weather will stay constant. It won't be until two air masses meet that you will notice changes in the weather at the front that marks the meeting place.

Air masses can be cold and dry, hot and dry, cool and moist, or warm and moist. It all depends upon the surface conditions when the mass forms. In the United States, we experience air masses with bitter cold and dry air, warm air with a lot of moisture, cold weather moving slowly with some precipitation, and warm and dry air masses.

If a dry air mass lingers over an area with crops that need water to grow, or a bitterly cold air mass lingers over any area at all, the people in that area are well aware of the effects. Those at the front

Let's Talk About the Weather

of air masses are also aware of the meeting of those air masses when they produce extreme weather conditions.[2]

Tornadoes

A tornado is a violent column of air. It reaches down from a thunderstorm to the ground. It rotates and moves. A powerful tornado can have wind speeds of up to 300 miles (483 km) per

Tornadoes are often described as funnel clouds. They stretch from the clouds to the ground, rotating as they move rapidly through an area.

Earth Science in Your Everyday Life

hour. These tornados can do an incredible amount of damage—destroying buildings and tossing cars and trucks around. A tornado can rotate and travel up to 50 miles (80.5 km) before its energy is dissipated. It can be as wide as a mile (1.6 km).

Tornadoes are unpredictable, but we do know that certain conditions make it more likely than others for a tornado to occur. These conditions are when warm, humid air from the Gulf of Mexico meets cool, dry air from Canada. As these air masses meet, conditions in the atmosphere become unstable. The wind changes direction as the wind speed increases. The height of the weather also changes as it moves higher and creates a spinning effect in the lower atmosphere. You cannot see this spinning air.[3]

The air continues to rise. This rising air causes the air to stop rotating horizontally and to begin rotating vertically. The result of

What Causes a Thunderstorm?

Thunderstorms are a frequent occurrence in much of the United States. They are the starting point for tornadoes in some parts of the country. In others areas, they are the whole story. Thunderstorms are formed when warm air rises from the surface of Earth. This warm air then cools and the colder air sinks. This up and down movement of warm and cold air is called a convection current. If a cold front is moving in, the much colder air in that air mass causes the warm air to rise much higher than it normally would. Convection currents, combined with condensation in the form of rain, create a thunderstorm.[4]

Let's Talk About the Weather

Lightning is the result of positive and negative charges building up within a storm cloud. The two charges ignite a huge spark.

this rising air is an area of rotation that can be up to 6 miles (10 km) wide. This area is where tornadoes can form. Sometimes you might see a funnel cloud, a rotating cone of air that reaches down to the ground from a thunderstorm. This isn't a tornado, but if it touches the ground, it will become a tornado.

Earth Science in Your Everyday Life

Tornadoes are more common in some areas of Earth than others. This is because you must have the combination of moist, warm air like that moving in from the Gulf of Mexico meeting very dry air like that moving down from Canada. Without those conditions, there is no threat of a tornado. For those who live in areas where there is a strong chance of tornadoes, there are sirens that sound when the air begins to rotate. This gives people some time to head for a safe place. As we learn more about the atmosphere, we will be better able to predict these dangerous storms.

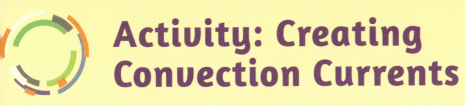

Activity: Creating Convection Currents

You read about thunderstorms and understand they are caused by the rapid rising and falling of warm, moist air and dry, cool air. Maybe you have seen birds of prey taking advantage of a column of warm air by using that upward motion to keep them aloft without flapping their wings. Or perhaps you live in an area where you can see the shimmering of hot air rising off of very hot pavement. These events occur because of convection currents. Make convection currents of your own!

The warm red-colored water and cold blue-colored water simulate hot and cold air in the atmosphere.

Earth Science in Your Everyday Life

Things You Will Need:

- **permission to handle very hot water**
- **blue food coloring**
- **an ice cube tray or small container**
- **a freezer**

- **a large clear rectangular container about 4 inches (10 cm) high**
- **water**
- **a small bottle or container**
- **red food coloring**
- **thermometer**

*Note: If you use small containers to freeze the ice or for the hot water, be sure the containers are small enough to sit in the larger rectangular container and have several inches of water above them.

■ **1.** Mix a few drops of blue food coloring with water.

■ **2.** Pour the blue water into an ice cube tray.

■ **3.** Put the tray in the freezer and wait until the ice is frozen.

■ **4.** Fill the rectangular container about three-quarters of the way full of room temperature water. Heat the water if necessary to reach a temperature of about 70°F (21°C).

■ **5.** Fill the small bottle about three-quarters full of very hot water.

■ **6.** Add enough red food coloring to it to make the water look really red. Be sure the water in this bottle is at least 95°F (35°C).

Let's Talk About the Weather

■ **7.** At the same time, put a blue ice cube in one end of the large rectangular container, and, keeping your finger over the opening, put the bottle of hot red liquid in the water at the other end of the large rectangular container.

■ **8.** Remove your finger from the opening.

The water from the red container first floats at the top and then sinks to the bottom of the container as it cools to a temperature that is less than the temperature of the water in the large container. The melting water from the blue ice cube first sinks to the bottom and then rises to the top of the container as the water warms to the temperature of the water in the large container.

You will see the colors mixing as they meet each other and cool or heat to the temperature of the large container. Eventually the water in the large container will turn purple as the red and blue water mixes completely when the red and blue water reach the same temperature as the water in the large container. This activity is the same sort of activity a warm air mass and a cold air mass experience when they meet at a front.

The Earth-Sun-Moon System

NASA defines astronomy as the study of stars, planets, and space. We study these celestial bodies and their environment to find answers to questions of how the world began, whether we are the only species like ours in the universe, and if Earth is moving away from the planets around it.

Celestial Bodies

The universe is home to many celestial bodies. There are planets, galaxies, and stars, to name a few. A planet is a body that moves in an elliptical orbit around a star, which in our case, is the sun. A planet also has to be round, cannot be a satellite of another object, and its orbit path must be free of debris.[1]

You usually need a telescope to get a good look at a planet because planets are not nearby. You can see stars on any clear night. The less light there is around you, the more stars you can observe because the light from the ground doesn't interfere. Many stars are in constellations, groups that are often named after animals and mythological figures.

While both planets and stars have mass and are nearly round, stars are fixed points in the sky. They are not orbiting anything. A star is usually a body of gas that creates nuclear fusion because it is large and dense enough that heat and crushing pressure combine to produce this energy.

A galaxy is a star system comprised of millions or billions of stars held together by gravity. Earth is part of the Milky Way galaxy. The sun is at the center of our galaxy. Sometimes, on a summer night, in a very dark place, you can get a glimpse of one arm of the Milky Way without the use of a telescope. The stars you see overhead every night are also part of the Milky Way.

When considering the start of our universe, scientists wondered whether or not the stars were moving apart. This was important to the big bang theory, which says that everything was created in an instant from one central point and has been moving rapidly apart for billions of years. Astronomers are still at work, using ever more sophisticated space telescopes and imaging devices, to find evidence to support or contradict this theory.

Edwin Hubble, Cepheid Variables, and the One-Galaxy Theory

In the early 1900s, astronomer Edwin Hubble (1889–1953) used a large telescope to study a special type of star called a Cepheid variable and proved that there is more than one galaxy in the universe. This type of star cycles between growing brighter and dimmer on a regular schedule. The maximum brightness is the same for each of these stars. By using a telescope to study how luminous different Cepheid variable stars appeared, Hubble could calculate the distance to those stars. These calculations helped him show that the stars he observed were in a different galaxy from our own.

Earth Science in Your Everyday Life

Astronomic Processes in Action

In our everyday lives, we are most concerned with events on Earth that are caused by the interaction of Earth, the moon, and the sun.

Tides

On a daily basis, the moon interacts with our oceans to cause tides. The moon has the greatest effect on the tides because it is closer than the sun. As the moon orbits the sun, the gravity of the moon creates a tidal force that causes the water on Earth to bulge out on the sides closest to and farthest from the moon. When your location enters a bulge, the tide is high. When your location exits a bulge, the tide is low.

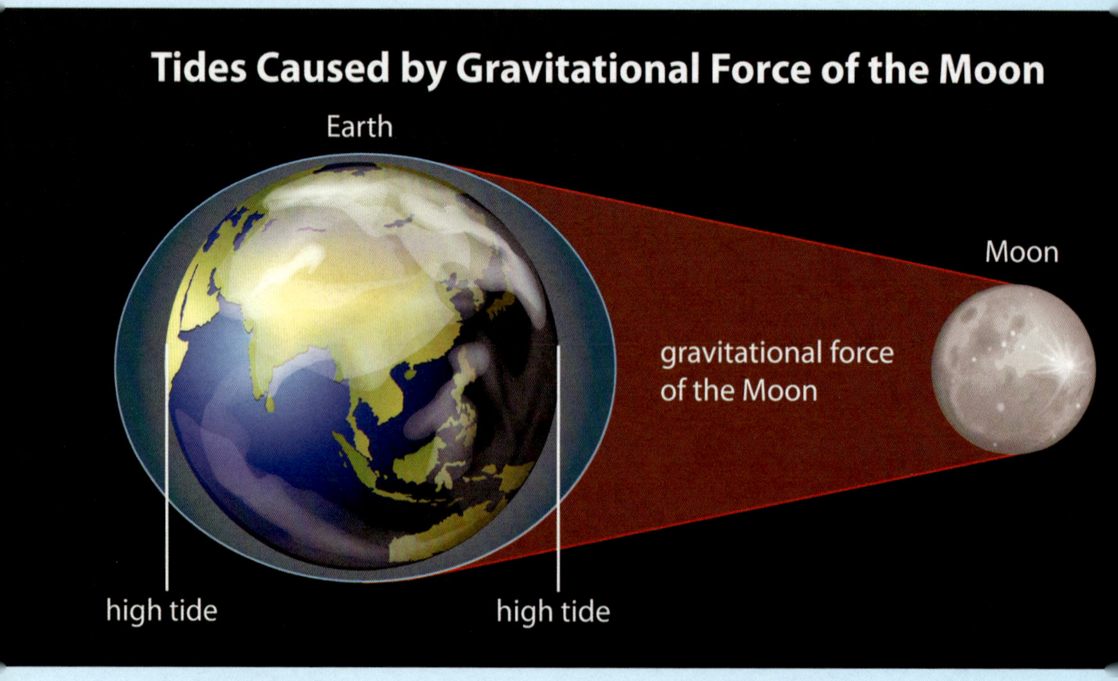

Tides Caused by Gravitational Force of the Moon

Earth

gravitational force of the Moon

Moon

high tide   high tide

The changing tides are due to the gravitational pull of the moon upon Earth.

The Earth-Sun-Moon System

Seasons

The seasons are cyclical changes in weather patterns and hours of daylight. These changes (winter, spring, summer, fall) are caused by Earth's position relative to the sun. The seasons are caused by the tilt of Earth in combination with its orbit of the sun. It is not the same everywhere. When it is winter in the Northern Hemisphere, it is summer in the Southern Hemisphere. The reverse is true, too. And spring and fall occur at opposite times as well.

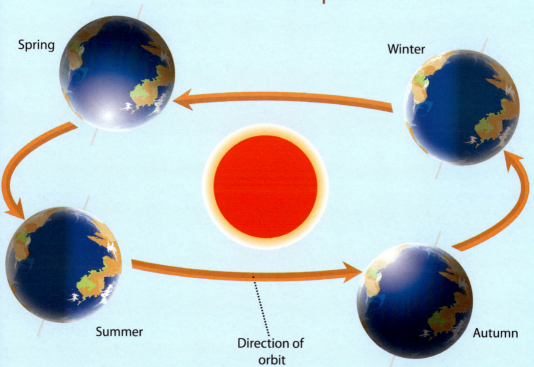

As Earth makes its annual cycle around the sun, the seasons change according to Earth's position relative to the sun.

Earth Science in Your Everyday Life

The constants are the position of the sun and the angle of the tilt. During the Northern Hemisphere's winter, the tilt causes the Southern Hemisphere to receive the direct rays of the sun. As a result, December is a summer month there. During the Northern Hemisphere's summer, the tilt causes the sun's rays to shine directly on this part of the world. As a result, June is a summer month in the Northern Hemisphere but a winter month in the Southern Hemisphere. During the spring and fall, the Earth's tilt and its position relative to the sun cause the sun's rays to hit both hemispheres equally.[2]

Eclipses

There are two types of eclipses that we can see from Earth. One type is known as a solar eclipse. The other is known as a lunar eclipse. Both occur when Earth, the sun, and the moon are in a straight line. Solar eclipses form when the new moon moves between the sun and Earth.

Lunar eclipses form when Earth moves between the sun and the full moon. Earth blocks the sun's rays from reflecting off the moon and dims the light of the full moon.[3]

Day and Night

Day and night are two other results of astronomical events. The sun remains constant, but Earth is always in orbit around the sun. If Earth never spun on its axis and always showed just one side to the sun, that side would always be in daylight. A full spin around the axis takes about twenty-four hours. This span of time is what we call a day.

When Earth turns the surface where we live toward the sun, it is daylight, but daylight doesn't suddenly appear on an entire side of Earth. You can see this for yourself if you speak to someone

The Earth-Sun-Moon System

in California when you are in New York. The sun will appear in New York first and make its appearance across the country until it reaches California. Actually, the sun has not reached anywhere. It is Earth that has spun your location out of the path of the sun.

You can check with the person in California and you will learn that the sun rises in California approximately three hours after it rises on the East Coast.

Activity: Building a Solar Oven

People can use the sun to heat their houses. Some can even use solar power ovens to cook their food!

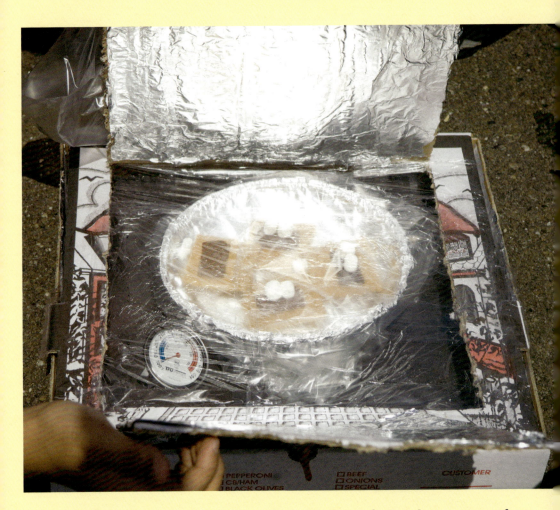

Students in New York built a solar oven out of pizza boxes to cook s'mores. The activity on the next page uses a similar approach to cook eggs.

The Earth-Sun-Moon System

Things You Will Need:

- 3 empty pizza boxes
- a glue stick
- 4 pieces of aluminum foil (10 inches [25 cm] each)
- 3 pieces of aluminum foil (4 inches [10 cm] each)
- a piece of plastic wrap (10 inches [25 cm]) plus extra

- a mirror that is about 10 inches (25 cm) long
- 3 uncooked eggs
- a small bowl
- a whisk or fork
- 3 paint stirrers or rulers
- masking tape

■ **1.** Open the pizza boxes on a table. Glue the 10-inch pieces of aluminum foil to the inside of the bottom of all three.

■ **2.** Glue the last 10-inch piece of aluminum foil to the inside of the top of one box.

■ **3.** Glue the 10-inch plastic wrap to the inside top of another box.

■ **4.** Glue the mirror to the inside top of the last box.

■ **5.** Use the three 4-inch pieces of aluminum foil to make a small bowl for each egg.

■ **6.** Beat each egg in the small bowl that you did NOT make.

Earth Science in Your Everyday Life

■ **7.** Pour the egg into a small bowl that you did make. Do this for each egg.

■ **8.** Find a flat place outside in direct sunlight—about an hour past noon would be best. Place each of the small bowls on the bottom foil of each box. Make sure the bowl you made is steady. Put plastic wrap over the entire box bottoms, covering the eggs.

■ **9.** Use the paint stirrers or rulers to keep the tops of the boxes partly open at an angle toward the sun. Use the masking tape to make it so that the box tops stay in place.

■ **10.** Leave the eggs and boxes for three hours.

What do you see in each box? If one set of materials cooked the egg faster than the others, explain why. If none of the eggs cooked at all, why might that be?

The shiny surfaces of the aluminum foil and mirror reflect the sunlight into the box, which then heats the air trapped inside by the plastic wrap, cooking the eggs. This works better in the summertime, when the sun's rays hit directly.

Cycles in Action

Chapter 5

A cycle is an event that repeats itself on a regular basis unless there is interference. You are aware that a day is a twenty-four-hour cycle and a year is a cycle of approximately 365 days. Four important cycles on Earth are the rock cycle, the water cycle, the nitrogen cycle, and the carbon cycle. Each of these cycles has inputs and outputs that keep them going.

The Rock Cycle

You would need hundreds of years to witness a complete rock cycle on a large scale. This cycle is basic to geology and explains how the different types of rock have come to be. In the rock cycle, weathering by mechanical or chemical means, along with erosion caused by water, wind, or other natural processes, breaks down the igneous, sedimentary, and metamorphic rock on Earth's surface. You can see this process in action when you observe the changes in rocks after a winter with wet, freezing weather. Usually the expansion of the water as ice is formed will push the sides of the rock apart and result in cracks or fissures.

The eroded pieces of rock are then transported by wind or precipitation and deposited in a layer that is higher than the base layer. The bottom layer of this sedimentary material is exposed to pressure from the layers above. Over time, they form sedimentary rock. Over many years, this sedimentary rock may be covered far underground. Exposed to pressure and heat there, it will form metamorphic rock. (You will not see this process because the rock must move very far underground before this metamorphism

Earth Science in Your Everyday Life

Concepts in Geology

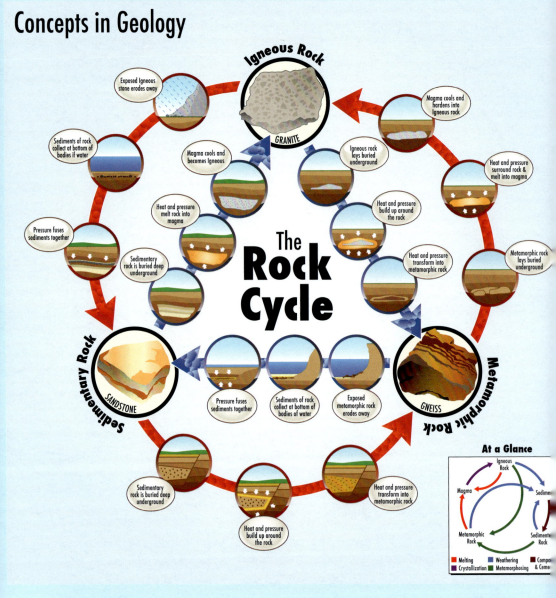

Without the rock cycle, every surface beneath your feet would be a solid block of rock of unchanging depth. This diagram shows how rock is formed and then broken down.

Cycles in Action

occurs.) When the metamorphic rock moves deep enough, it will melt to become the magma we see as lava escapes from a volcano. The lava cools and forms igneous rock.

Now the cycle repeats itself with the available igneous, sedimentary, and metamorphic rock. If you want to observe part of the process—either the input or the output—you can search for different types of rock. These will help you to know what step of the rock cycle you are observing.[1]

The Water Cycle

The water cycle, also known as the hydrological or hydrologic cycle, moves water between Earth's oceans, atmosphere, and land—and back again. During the cycle, the water may take the form of rain or snow. It may take the form of water that enters streams, brooks, or rivers. It may travel through evaporation or transpiration, the release of water into the atmosphere by plants. The water cycle is an important part of our weather, as well.

The steps of the water cycle are evaporation, condensation, precipitation, and collection in a continuous series of steps. The sun shines on bodies of water. The heat turns the water into a vapor that rises to the sky. It's colder in the sky, so the vapor condenses into droplets. These droplets fall to Earth as precipitation such as of rain, snow, or hail—depending on the temperature—due to the force of gravity. The water is soaked into the ground to become part of the water cycle or runs off into streams, brooks, or rivers and is collected. The sun shines on bodies of water and the heat of the sun turns that water into water vapor. And the cycle begins again.

If temperatures are too hot or there is not enough rain to collect efficiently, the water cycle does not work well and there are drought conditions. When there is too much precipitation,

Earth Science in Your Everyday Life

PHOTOSYNTHESIS

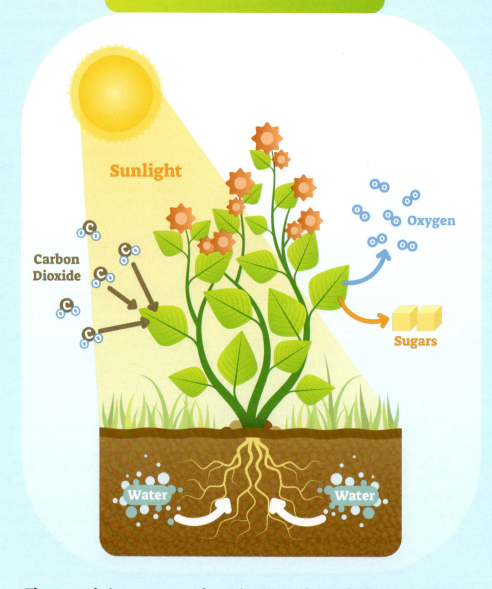

The roots bring water and nutrients up through the stem. Energy from the sun converts water and carbon dioxide into oxygen and sugars (glucose).

Cycles in Action

Photosynthesis

In photosynthesis, green plants make their own food by converting light energy into chemical energy. During the cycle, water is sucked up from the soil through the root system and stem. The sun's rays shine on the green leaves. The work of photosynthesis takes place within the leaves when water and carbon dioxide are present. The leaves have small pores called stomata that open to let carbon dioxide enter. At the same time, water is lost though the stomata. The outputs from this cycle are oxygen and glucose (carbohydrates). The oxygen is released. Some of the glucose is used for the plant to grow. The rest stays in the leaves as starch that serves as food for animals that eat the leaves.[2]

the collection part of the cycle becomes overfilled and there are floods. When conditions are just right, the cycle works as it should and plants, humans, and animals have the water they need.[3]

The Nitrogen Cycle

The nitrogen cycle is the cycle by which nitrogen moves between plants, animals, bacteria, the atmosphere, and the land. It is necessary for nitrogen to change forms several times so that everything that requires nitrogen can access the nitrogen it needs.

Earth Science in Your Everyday Life

THE NITROGEN CYCLE

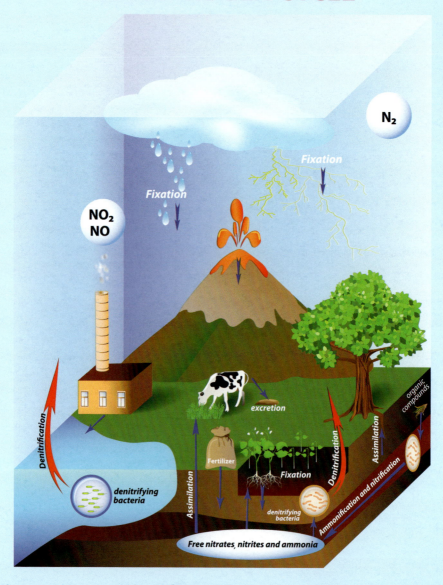

Nitrogen is essential to life, but plants and animals cannot get it from the atmosphere. Plants must get it through the processes of fixation and nitrification performed by bacteria. Then animals eat the plants to get their nitrogen.

Cycles in Action

When a plant or animal dies, decomposers such as bacteria and fungi break it down. Bacteria change nitrogen into ammonium in the fixation stage. Bacteria then turn the ammonium into a form of nitrogen—nitrates—that can be absorbed by plants during the nitrification phase. The plants absorb the nitrates through their root system. It is then used in amino acids, nucleic acids, and chlorophyll within the plant and leaves during the assimilation phase. When the plant or animal that ate the plant dies, bacteria and fungi turn the nitrogen back into ammonium. The cycle begins again.

If there is too much nitrogen in the soil, green plants will have lots of green leaves but very few flowers or fruit. It would also hurt the roots of the plants. If there is too little nitrogen in the soil, the plants will be yellow and withered. They also will not grow as much as they should. As is the case in the other cycles, the materials entering the cycle and those produced by the cycle must be in a balance. When they are not, the cycle will not work.

You see the nitrogen cycle in action when you see great fields of corn or wheat. Those crops could not grow without the correct amount of nitrogen.[4]

The Carbon Cycle

The carbon cycle is vital to Earth's climate. This is the cycle that determines the temperatures that affect climate. When there is too much carbon dioxide in the atmosphere, the carbon dioxide traps heat in the atmosphere. Global climate change is a noticeable indicator that the carbon cycle on Earth is not working properly. We are producing too much carbon dioxide. Plants cannot photosynthesize quickly enough to produce oxygen from all that carbon dioxide.

Earth Science in Your Everyday Life

In the carbon cycle, burning of fossil fuels, the decay of plants and animals, and respiration by animals and humans releases carbon dioxide into the atmosphere. Photosynthesis uses some of that carbon dioxide to produce starch and oxygen. Carbon dioxide in the air is also used by phytoplankton and found in sinking sediment and circulated deep in the ocean.

This is one cycle that you can definitely witness and have a part in during a lifetime. As more fossil fuels are burned, more animals are raised on land that used to be forests, and more wildfire activity happens, the load of carbon dioxide in the atmosphere increases. You can help this cycle stay in balance by reducing your use of fossil fuels and making sure that vast areas of forests are preserved or replanted.[5]

Activity: A Terrarium with Cycles

Photosynthesis is an important cycle that deserves a bit more attention. Let's use what you know of photosynthesis to produce some water from the plants near your school or home.

If it is summer and you live in an area with green leafy trees, try this.

Things You Will Need:

- a clear jumbo plastic bag
- a green, leafy branch
- rope to tie the bag closed
- a sunny day

■ **1.** Take the bag and put it over the leafy branch so that the branch is inside the bag but not completely filling the bag.

■ **2.** Tie the bag tightly shut.

■ **3.** Leave it alone in a sunny place and return in about two hours. How did the water get into the bag?

Earth Science in Your Everyday Life

If it is winter or you don't live near green leafy trees, try this.

Things You Will Need:

- a large, clean, clear glass container
- enough potting soil to cover the bottom of the container about ¼ full
- a small plant
- paper towel for any messes
- ½ cup (118 mL) of water
- enough plastic wrap to cover the top of the container
- a large rubber band to keep the plastic wrap securely on the top of the glass container
- a sunny place or a lamp with a bulb

■ 1. Put the dirt in the container and put the plant in the dirt. Clean the sides of the container if you got them really dirty.

■ 2. Pour some water on the soil, but don't soak it.

■ 3. Put the plastic wrap over the top of the container and use the rubber band for a tight seal.

■ 4. Leave it in the sun or in the lamp light for a day.

■ 5. Check back. Write what you observe. Do this for three days.

What do you see? Is there any water at the top or sides of the container? Where did it come from?

Cycles in Action

During photosynthesis, as carbon dioxide enters the leaves though the stomata, water escapes as vapor in a process called transpiration. The water vapor gets trapped in the plastic bag or the tightly sealed glass container and changes back to liquid form as condensation.

Chapter Notes

■ Chapter 1
The Earth Beneath Your Feet

1. Elizabeth Howell, "Earth's Core 1,000 Degrees Hotter Than Expected," LiveScience, April 25, 2013, https://www.livescience.com/29054-earth-core-hotter.html.
2. "What Are Fossil Fuels?" BELCO, https://belco.bm/index.php/education-86/what-are-fossil-fuels (accessed September 2, 2018).
3. Jeannie Evers, ed., "Ring of Fire," National Geographic, updated January 6, 2015, https://www.nationalgeographic.org/encyclopedia/ring-fire/.
4. Becky Oskin, "What Is Plate Tectonics?" LiveScience, December 19, 2017, https://www.livescience.com/37706-what-is-plate-tectonics.html.
5. "Earthquakes," USGS, https://earthquake.usgs.gov/earthquakes/ (accessed September 2, 2018).

■ Chapter 2
The Oceans Around You

1. "Ocean Currents," NOAA, https://www.noaa.gov/resource-collections/ocean-currents (accessed September 2, 2018).
2. "Rip Currents," NOAA, https://www.weather.gov/media/safety/ripcurrent_faqs.pdf (accessed September 2, 2018).
3. Heather Greenwood Davis, "Bay of Fundy," National Geographic, https://www.nationalgeographic.com/travel/canada/bay-

Chapter Notes

of-fundy-new-brunswick-nova-scotia/ (accessed September 22, 2018).

4. "What Are Tides?" NOAA, updated June 25, 2018, https://oceanservice.noaa.gov/facts/tides.html.

5. "Hurricanes, Tropical Storms and Tropical Depressions: The Life Cycle of a Tropical System," ABC 7, October 3, 2018, https://abc7ny.com/weather/the-life-cycle-of-a-hurricane/1544248/.

6. Rebecca Hersher, "Climate Change Drives Bigger, Wetter Storms—Storms Like Florence," NPR, September 11, 2018, https://www.npr.org/2018/09/11/646313648/climate-change-drives-bigger-wetter-storms-storms-like-florence.

■ Chapter 3
Let's Talk About the Weather

1. "Air Masses and Fronts," University of Wisconsin, https://cimss.ssec.wisc.edu/wxwise/class/frntmass.html (accessed October 2, 2018).

2. Kim Rutledge, et al, "Air Mass," National Geographic, updated March 30, 2011, https://www.nationalgeographic.org/encyclopedia/air-mass/.

3. "Tornadoes," Weather WizKids, http://www.weatherwizkids.com/weather-tornado.htm (accessed October 4, 2018).

4. "What Causes Thunderstorms?" NASA, https://pmm.nasa.gov/education/content/what-causes-thunderstorms (accessed September 18, 2018).

■ Chapter 4
The Earth-Sun-Moon System

1. Elizabeth Howell, "What Is a Planet?" Space.com, April 6, 2018, https://www.space.com/25986-planet-definition.html.

Earth Science in Your Everyday Life

2. "What Causes the Seasons?" NASA Space Place, updated October 27, 2016, https://spaceplace.nasa.gov/seasons/en/.
3. "What Is an Eclipse?" NASA, updated August 6, 2017, https://www.nasa.gov/audience/forstudents/5-8/features/nasa-knows/what-is-an-eclipse-58.

■ Chapter 5
Cycles in Action

1. Isaac Harder, "The Rock Cycle," Mineralogy4Kids, http://www.mineralogy4kids.org/?q=rock-cycle (accessed October 2, 2018).
2. Aparna Vidyasagar, "What Is Photosynthesis?" LiveScience, October 15, 2018, https://www.livescience.com/51720-photosynthesis.html.
3. "Water Cycle," NASA, https://pmm.nasa.gov/education/water-cycle (accessed October 7, 2018).
4. "The Nitrogen Cycle," Ducksters, https://www.ducksters.com/science/ecosystems/nitrogen_cycle.php (accessed October 6, 2018).
5. Holli Riebeek, "The Carbon Cycle," NASA Earth Observatory, June 16, 2011, https://earthobservatory.nasa.gov/Features/CarbonCycle.

assimilation The phase in the nitrogen cycle in which plants and animals take in nitrogen.

convection current A pattern of warm air rising from Earth's surface, cooling, and then sinking.

Coriolis effect The force created by Earth's rotation that makes currents and other moving objects travel at a curve and is responsible for making them move to the right in the Northern Hemisphere and to the left in the Southern Hemisphere.

debris Remains of destroyed structures.

decomposer An organism, such as a bacterium or fungus, that breaks down dead plants and animals.

deposit To pick up material from one location and leave it somewhere else.

erosion The process in which water or wind transports rock or other material from one location to another.

fixation The phase in the nitrogen cycle in which bacteria changes nitrogen into ammonium.

luminous Full of light.

nitrification The phase in the nitrogen cycle in which bacteria turn ammonium into a form of nitrogen—nitrates—that can be absorbed by plants.

nuclear fusion The type of energy used by stars to create light and heat.

phytoplankton Microscopic plants that float in the ocean.

surf zone The area on a coast where the waves break on the shore.

terrarium A clear container where plants are kept.

transpiration The evaporation of water into the atmosphere through the stomata of plants.

weathering The breaking down of rock or other material by air, water, or organisms.

Further Reading

Books

Cummings, Judy Dodge. *Earth, Wind, Fire, and Rain: Real Tales of Temperamental Elements.* New York, NY: Nomad Press, 2018.

Gardner, Robert, and Joshua Conklin. *Experiments for Future Meteorologists.* New York, NY: Enslow Publishing, 2017.

Idzikowski, Lisa. *Ecology in Your Everyday Life.* New York, NY: Enslow Publishing, 2019.

Sidabras, Kimberly. *Oceans.* Philadelphia, PA: Mason Crest Publishers, 2018.

Washburne, Sophie. *Alternative Energy Sources: The End of Fossil Fuels?* New York, NY: Lucent Books, 2019.

Websites

NASA Earth Science
science.nasa.gov/earth-science
Learn more about weather, climate change, Earth's cycles, and other topics of earth science.

National Oceanic and Atmospheric Administration (NOAA)
www.noaa.gov
Read the latest news on weather, oceanography, and climate.

US Geological Survey (USGS)
www.usgs.gov
Explore real-time data and information on natural hazards such as earthquakes, volcanic eruptions, and landslides.

Index

A
air mass, 28, 30, 31, 32
astronomic processes, 40–43
astronomy, 4, 38
atmosphere, 4, 28, 32, 34, 49, 51, 53, 54
axis, 42

B
bacteria, 51, 53
Bay of Fundy, 21
beaches, 19, 22, 24–25
    activity, 26–27
big bang theory, 39

C
carbon cycle, 47, 53–54
celestial bodies, 21, 38–39
Cepheid variable, 39
climate, 19, 21, 53
convection current, 4, 32
Coriolis effect, 17
currents, 17–19
cycle, 4, 17, 39, 47–54
    activity, 55–57

D
day and night, 42–43

decomposer, 52, 53

E
Earth, 4, 6, 7, 10, 11, 12, 17, 21, 24, 28, 32, 34, 38, 40, 41, 42, 43, 47, 49, 53
    activity, 14–16
    layers of, 7–9
earthquakes, 4, 7, 11, 13
earth science, 4–6, 28
    different fields of, 4, 6
earth-sun-moon system, 38–43
    activity, 44–46
eclipses, 42
erosion, 4, 47

F
fixation, 53
fossil fuels, 4, 9, 54
front, 4, 30, 32

G
galaxy, 38, 39
geology, 4, 7, 47
global climate change, 22, 53

H
Hubble, Edwin, 39
hurricane, 21–22, 24, 25

63

Earth Science in Your Everyday Life

M
metamorphism, 47, 49
meteorology, 4, 28

N
nitrification, 53
nitrogen cycle, 47, 51–53
Northern Hemisphere, 17, 41, 42
nuclear fusion, 38

O
oceanography, 4, 17
oceans, 4, 7, 17–25, 40, 49
one-galaxy theory, 39

P
Pangea, 12
photosynthesis, 51, 54
phytoplankton, 54
planets, 4, 38
plate tectonics, 12–13
precipitation, 30, 47, 49

R
Ring of Fire, 11
rip currents, 19
rock cycle, 47, 49

S
seasons, 41–42
Southern Hemisphere, 17, 41, 42
surf zone, 19

T
thunderstorm, 31, 32, 33
tides, 4, 19, 21, 22, 24, 40
tornado, 31–34
transpiration, 49
tropical storms, 21–22, 25

V
volcano, 4, 7, 9–11, 49

W
water cycle, 4, 47, 49, 51
weather, 4, 28, 32, 41, 47, 49
    activity, 35–37
    causes of, 28, 30–31
weathering, 47